Don't Piss In My SANCTUARY!

A Call to Protect the Power of the Message

Cederick L. Moore

Published By:
Jasher Press & Co.
www.jasherpress.com
customerservice@jasherpress.com
1.888.220.2068
New Bern, NC 28561

Copyright© 2014
Interior Text Design by Pamela S. Almore
Cover Design by Pamela S. Almore

ISBN: **9780692021965**

All rights reserved. Except for brief excerpts used in reviews, no portion of this work may be reproduced or published without expressed written permission from the author or the author's agent.

All scriptures are taken from the King James version of the Holy Bible.

First Edition
Printed and bound in the United States of America

JASHER PRESS & CO.

DEDICATION

I dedicate this book to all servants of God who desire to serve Him out of a pure conscience. Continue to defend the truth. Our message is no longer popular, but it is necessary for deliverance and Christian growth. Don't give up; your reward is in Heaven.

FOREWORD

"Pastor Moore has undoubtedly pushed the magnitude of transparency and preaching motive hidden by the majority of today's preachers off the cliff and into the waters of exposure with no life jacket. Don't Piss In My Sanctuary opens a shut door that has been closed by preachers and is evidence that Pastor Moore stands on the razor's edge. This book will cause you to subject yourself to the exposure, admit, bow to repentance, and humble yourself for transformation. After reading this book, I can assure you that your motive for ministry will change along with your focus in the midst of ministry persecutions."

-Elder Aaron B. McNair, Jr.
AMJ Ministries
Greenville, NC

Table of Contents

- Introduction 11
- Words of Power 15
- Examine Your Words 25
- Walk Through the Fire 35
- Words of Retaliation 41
- Sympathy-Seeking Words 49
- of Bitterness 49
- Words of Mind Control 57
- Final Words 63
- Concluding Prayer 67
- About the Author 69

INTRODUCTION

A few weeks before God established the church that I pastor, *Spirit & Truth Cathedral of Fire*, I experienced a captivating dream. In that dream, I was carefully preparing a message in my study when I recognized it was time for me to enter the sanctuary. Upon this recognition, I closed my sermon portfolio and proceeded to enter the presence of the Lord. The congregation sang and danced as I made my virtually unnoticed entrance from a side door. I made my way to the back of the church, looked around, and basked in the warmth of the worship as it went forth as a sweet savor into the nostrils of God. After a few seconds, I looked around and became fixated on an electrical outlet in a pillar in the middle of the aisle. I then did the unthinkable; still unnoticed by the congregation, I began to urinate in that electrical socket. I plugged in the cord of undistinguishable equipment in the same socket after I relieved myself. Immediately a spark shot out and an ominous fire commenced. Upon recognizing the fire, I heard a voice from above my head say, "Don't piss in my sanctuary." It is my personal conviction that that voice belonged to the Holy Spirit—He who guides, comforts, convicts, and teaches every believer.

This book is what I perceive the Holy Spirit was conveying to me with those words of admonition. In it you will find discussions of common pitfalls of ministers that cause them to have piss sessions in God's sanctuary. I will provide possible recourses to take instead so that God can continually be glorified and the saints of God edified. As you read forward, I pray that the fire of God burns in your soul and that you experience deliverance, refreshment, and inspiration of some sort. I pray that it grounds you in your life commitment as a flame of fire for the Lord Jesus Christ. Thank God for his grace and mercy, for if it had not been for them, even we would have been consumed by his righteous indignation.

CHAPTER 1

WORDS OF POWER

"Death and life are in the power of the tongue, and they that love it shall eat the fruit thereof."
—Proverbs 18:21

In the natural sense, urination is a vital, voluntary process for most people. It is during this process that excess water and waste materials are removed from the blood and discharged from the body. Sicknesses and ultimately death are the results of urination obstruction. As it is in the natural, so it is in the spiritual sense. Spiritual sicknesses and death are the results of deliverance obstruction. The Bible teaches us that "many are the afflictions of the righteous…" (Psalm 34:19). In every affliction, there are lessons for believers to absorb and all forms of negativity that need to be removed from our consciousness and discharged through the water of God's Word. Without this process, many of us, especially ministers, will get sick and die—spiritual or even natural deaths. As the strength of our spirits wane, so will the effectiveness of our gospel message. Therefore, we ministers require proper channels to relieve ourselves of negative energies; however, proper channels do not include our pulpits.

The proper channels ministers need embrace during mental and emotional duress include but are not limited to God in prayer, a spiritually mature confidante, a consistent exercise program, rest and relaxation, and mental health professionals. I advise mental health professionals with caution, because I believe mental health is a matter of the spirit and perspective that can be remedied within the

Kingdom. If Paul took offense to Christians going to secular judges to solve problems amongst the people of God, is not it only right to take offense to the idea of Christians seeking mental health therapy from potential unbelievers (1 Corinthians 6:1-8)? The shame that Paul accentuates in the aforementioned Corinthian text is the idea of Christians subjecting themselves to the moral evaluation of unbelievers—people who need to see Christians living out the love of Jesus faithfully. Similarly, Christians who seek help from mental health professionals indirectly subject themselves to moral evaluation by unbelievers. Of course, the previous commentary assumes that the Christian is not seeking help from a Christian psychologist or psychiatrist. I do believe God is calling forth compassionate Christians who are taking leadership roles and careers in the field of Christian psychology. Now more than ever, they are needed, because Satan has launched a vicious attack against those who are in covenant with God, "but the people that do know their God shall be strong, and do exploits" (Daniel 11:32) by all means necessary.

Ministers should not use the pulpit to relieve themselves of negative energies because the pulpit is a sacred desk that God intends for us to use for the "perfecting of the saints, for the work of the ministry, for the edifying of the body of Christ till we all come in the unity of the faith and of the knowledge of the Son of God, unto a perfect man, unto the measure of the stature of the fullness of Christ that we henceforth be no more children, tossed to and fro, and carried about with every wind of doctrine, by the sleight of men, and cunning craftiness, whereby they lie in wait to deceive; but speaking the truth in love, may grow up into him in all things, which is the head, even Christ" (Ephesians 4: 12-15). A key phrase in the previously quoted text is "speaking the truth in love." Love should be the motivating factor behind communication with God's people—love not retaliation or a tendency to "set the record straight." The full intention of an act of love is to facilitate life and wholeness, but words stemming from sinister hearts normally have corrupt results (Proverbs 10:11). As Jesus restored Peter in right standing with him, he demanded that Peter demonstrate his love for him by teaching believers the Word of God (John 21:15-17). From this biblical witness, we see that Christ associates love with the ministry of teaching and preaching. It takes love to nurture and protect God's people who to this day struggle with the spirit of variance. Our love for Christ must always shape our words and actions with regard to his people and the work of the ministry.

Ministers need not make the mistake of assuming that their words are negative or unwise just because people do not receive them with joy. Some responses to our words are just byproducts of satanic resistance and not a wrongly spoken word. In other words, ministers should not judge the results of their words solely on the responses of the people, because some people simply despise the truth. The book of Proverbs teaches us that the wise student of life knows that there are right words, right ways, and right times to speak. These ways and times should be respected; however, there are just some truths that will be offensive to certain people regardless of how or when they are communicated. Certain people will naturally be offended by the truth and oppose it vehemently so as to keep the light of God from shining on their wickedness. Jesus prepared us for this kind of reaction to corrective truth when he taught us saying, "For everyone that doeth evil hateth the light, neither cometh to the light, lest his deeds should be reproved" (John 3:20). Therefore, the verbal communication of order and correction is necessary, and it should not be equated to pissing in God's sanctuary per se.

The Bible teaches that ministers are to "preach the word; be instant in season and out of season; reprove, rebuke, exhort with all longsuffering and doctrine" (2 Timothy 4:2). And in another place, the Word teaches, "all scripture is given by inspiration of God, and is profitable for doctrine, for reproof, for correction, [and] for instruction in righteousness" (2 Timothy 3:16). The word of God is always right and is never wrong. Whether we are ready to accept it is irrelevant to the just standard of God's word. There are times when ministers must address specific sins that challenge vital administrative procedure, the system of life for the local congregation, or the agenda of the universal body of Christ. In this case, the saying, "them that sin rebuke before all, that others also may fear" is appropriately applied (I Timothy 5:20).

Many churches have become powerless laughingstocks because their leaders refuse to correct flagrant sin that undermines the work of the body of Christ. Some well-meaning leaders are apprehensive about correcting sin and disorder because of having seen this process perpetually abused. This line of thinking, however, is faulty and comparable to a parent not disciplining his child because his parents physically abused him. It may be uncomfortable to enforce a behavioral plan, but it is necessary to maintain divine order amongst the people of God. People are rebellious by nature, and there needs to be a trusted official in place that will uphold God's righteous standard of holiness.

Other ministers are hesitant to correct out of fear that people will no longer support them. Fear of correcting people's self-defeating behaviors opens the door to all kinds of spirits, namely among them, the spirit of manipulation and control. The Bible teaches us that "an open rebuke is better than hidden love" (Proverbs 27:5). In other words, ministers cannot allow the pain it causes us to correct God's people to keep us from opening our mouths and inflicting temporary pain to those who need the salvation of God's word.

Words mean everything, and it is time for people to hear that God knows the rebellion that is in our hearts and He is not pleased. Some well-meaning people will protest that people who err know they err and they need not hear someone correct them. They say things like, "Those who live lifestyles of sin know the err of their ways more than you do." Those words are diplomatic in nature and have their proper place to direct and shape our policies and procedures in disciplining God's people, but to use those ideas to quench God's zeal to uproot disobedience is wrong. The Scripture exhorts us to cry loud and spare not—to execute God's righteous judgment on that which is evil.

Love for people does not cancel out God's expectation for responsibility and accountability. Without the latter two distinguishing qualities, people run wild, thinking that they can do whatever they please without any divine consequences. It would be reckless for one to teach that order and correction is unwise—that it is condemning and self-righteous. Had Paul not brought order and correction to Early Christendom, we would not have most of the New Testament from which we read, learn, and grow, and much blood would have been on his hands. Corrected lives that maintain spiritual balance are necessary for us to produce life-giving fruit for desperate and destitute souls. Therefore, a minister must not solely base the worth or rightness of his words on human reactions to them and should be steadfast in being a defender of the truth.

CHAPTER 2

EXAMINE YOUR WORDS

"Let your speech always be with grace, seasoned with salt, that ye may know how ye ought to answer every man."
-Colossians 4:6

Whenever ministers are personally attacked, the responsible minister does well to vent outside of the pulpit and within the privacy of a quarantined environment. *We all know that ministers have flesh just as members of the laity do, but with the call to minister God's Word comes an elevated sense of responsibility and accountability with the words we speak and the actions we perform.* Consider the story of Moses to verify the previous claim. Moses, the deliverer of the Israelites, led the people of God out of bondage and into the wilderness to receive the Law of God and to prepare them to ascertain the promises of God for their lives. His compassion for these people was evident by the fact that he murdered an Egyptian taskmaster for beating one of them, judged between them at moments of contention, and interceded for them when God had enough of their waywardness. Even after being and doing all this for the people, God still denied Moses access to the Promised Land. Why would God do this? Plain and simple, Moses pissed in God's sanctuary.

At the beginning of Numbers 20, we see that the Israelites are congregated together to confront Moses about their unfortunate situation regarding the dearth of water to drink. The people of God came up against their leader, Moses, a mouthpiece for God. They expressed their discontent by saying that they wished they had died long before and that they believed that Moses had led them out of Egypt just to die of thirst and hunger in the wilderness (Numbers 20:3-5). The sin of the Israelites was a sin against God, and Moses allowed their problem to become his. The narrative continues in the following fashion: "And the LORD spake unto Moses saying, 'Take the rod, and gather thou the assembly together, thou, and Aaron thy brother, and speak ye unto the rock before their eyes; and it shall give forth his water, and thou shalt bring forth to them water out of the rock: so thou shalt give the congregation and their beasts drink.' And Moses took the rod from before the LORD, as he commanded him. And Moses and Aaron gathered the congregation together before the rock, and he said unto them, 'Hear now, ye rebels; must we fetch you water out of this rock?' And Moses lifted up his hand, and with his rod he smote the rock twice: and the water came out abundantly, and the congregation drank, and their beasts also. And the LORD spake unto Moses and Aaron, 'Because ye believed me not, to sanctify me in the eyes of the children of Israel, therefore ye shall not bring this congregation into the land which I have given them'" (Numbers 20:7-12).

Moses' anger and frustration with the people of God caused him to strike the rock twice instead of speaking to it as God had instructed him to do. His actions demonstrated his strength to the people instead of God's strength, and because of this, he was denied access into the Promised Land. This is what happens when ministers mount the podium to tell people off for personally offending them. They are striking people instead of speaking to them. They are demonstrating their strength instead of the strength of God. They allow the sins of the people to become their own by not focusing on what God has instructed them to do. They attempt to show how their flesh has more power to produce God's desired effect of change than actually does the grace and unadulterated Word of God. Moses' staff was a symbol for the Word of God. And although God's people are to be ruled with a rod of iron (Revelations 2:27), that rod should comfort (Psalm 23:4) a broken spirit and contrite heart (Psalm 51:17). That is essentially for why God uses our mouths, that is, to restore God's people to the quality of life that the Father has predestined for them to live.

The strength of the Word comes from its pure and uncompromising nature—not the aggressive spirit from which it is delivered. As ministers of the gospel, we must be ever so keenly aware of the effect of our mouths. The Scripture reads, "Death and life are in the power of the tongue, and they that love it shall eat the fruit thereof" (Proverbs 18:21). When people personally offend us, we have to take a minute, breathe, step back, and ask why we are in the soul-saving business. This mental break helps us keep our focus on the proper perspective of speaking life rather than condemnation. It will also reassure us of the time sensitive word that the Holy Spirit wants us to speak, whether it is a word of correction or encouragement.

A sure way of examining the kind of spirit we have is to get offended as people in authority and watch what we say in response to offenses. Consider Jesus' disciples' reactions to rejection, for example. After Samaritans rejected Jesus, James and John were livid, and they asked if they should call fire down from heaven to burn up them. (I conjecture that Peter's sporadic nature was tamed at this juncture of the journey, and that would explain his silence in the matter.) James and John were offended that their teacher was disrespected, and the only acceptable response for them was for them to kill their opposers.

In response to this, Jesus turned around and rebuked them saying, "Ye know not what manner of spirit ye are of. For the Son of man is not come to destroy men's lives, but to save them" (Luke 9:51-55). Just as Jesus told James and John, at times, Jesus has to turn around and tell us, yes, even us ministers, to "Shut up and check yourselves." Just because we have the credentials, experience, power, and platform, that does not give us a free pass to devastate the lives of people who offend us. We have made it this far in the Kingdom to speak life not destruction to those who oppose us.

Ministry is not for the fainthearted or thin-skinned. We must resist the urge to piss in God's sanctuary, for although relieving ourselves publically may feel good, the result does not yield the peaceable fruit of righteousness. And we must not make the mistake of thinking that getting back at people is the same thing as holding up God's righteous standard. Jesus is not as easily offended as we are, for God is love (1 John 4:8) and love is not easily angered (I Corinthians 13:5). As Christ's ambassadors, our words must coincide with the Spirit of Him who sent us.

Pissing in God's sanctuary can either prevent or delay people's entrance into their seasons of power and purpose, because instead of hearing the leading of God's voice through prophetic preaching, they are hearing poisonous venting sessions. The waiting congregation does not consist of all hired psychologists who get paid to hear ministers vent their frustrations about their family, employers, boss, self, church, or even God. They are like hungry and thirsty lambs that need quiet streams and green pastures from which to receive life-giving sustenance. They are like lost tourists who need directions in unfamiliar territories. They are like cancer patients who need emergency surgery to cut out self-destructive thought processes. They need to be shown how to take their afflictions and get out of them the nutrients they need to survive and thrive. They need an example to show them how to mature in Christ and throw away what is not necessary for life and godliness. If these people cannot receive this kind of critical help from spiritual leadership, what good are we to them? We would then be speaking ourselves into irrelevance. We would be as worthless salt thrown out and trodden under the feet of men.

CHAPTER 3

WALK THROUGH THE FIRE

"Every man's work shall be made manifest, for the day shall declare it, because it shall be revealed by fire; and the fire shall try every man's work of what sort it is."
- 1 Corinthians 3:13

The acidic quality of our venting may burn away the hope our congregants have for their situations. They may believe that if we cannot find any resolve in our own issues, neither can they. The oppressive spirit of frustration and bitterness will be transferred to the people through observational learning. People carefully observe us when we least expect them to do so. In fact, they watch more than they listen. So, we must be ever so careful to align our mouths with our actions, our actions with our professed lifestyle, and our lifestyle with the Word of God. As we model positive and scriptural responses to dealing with stress and disappointment, we will find God raising up mature believers in the sanctuary in which God has privileged us to serve. This is easier said than done, but we must apply ourselves to the Christian disciplines just as we require God's people to do so.

Most of us know the truth; we just decide to quench the Holy Spirit to satisfy the cravings of our flesh. With this idea in mind, it becomes evident why people piss in God's sanctuary even when they know that it is wrong. We, as ministers, must be willing to confront ourselves by beholding what we look like through the mirror of God's Word and do something about what we see. Oftentimes, many of us who carry God's word need deliverance ourselves. Many unclean spirits in us made it past the ministerial screening, and it is our responsibility to deal with these spirits that desire to quench the fire that Christ has ignited in our souls.

The word that has been communicated thus far has already separated the shepherds from the hirelings, the mature from the immature, and the honest from the dishonest. You who have continued to read and receive my words up to this present time are included in the third part of which God speaks of bringing through the fire. He says, "And I will bring the third part through the fire, and will refine them as silver is refined, and will try them as gold is tried: they shall call on my name, and I will hear them: I will say 'It is my people: and they shall say: The LORD is my God'" (Zechariah 13:9). God's ministers are to be as flames of fire (Psalm 104:4), and for that to be the case, the fire of His Spirit and Word must engulf us. We must report to work to speak what He wants to say to the body of Christ. It is when we sanctify God before the people that

God consumes our labor of love with fire, in other words, with power, signs, and wonders (I Kings 18:38, Mark 16:15-18). Let the truth of the matter resound: We are messengers of God. We speak on His behalf. His agenda is our agenda. He did not come to condemn the world, but that the world through him might be saved (John 3:7). Again, as his ambassadors, we should carry the same objective and spirit of mind.

The warning that is found within the title of this work does not negate the fact that there has been a lot of pissing going on in the house of God. Most of us who have persisted with the reading of this book have been guilty of this very thing from one degree to another. The continuous scattering of God's sheep is evidence of that fact, and God is not pleased with our pissing in his sanctuary. The saying holds true that when we know better, we should do better. Once we hear the word, we become accountable to what we have heard. I believe that in this hour, God is raising up a generation of prophetic voices who will obey the unction of the Holy Spirit. He is raising up people who know that it is only by God's grace that they are being used to such a capacity and that they have no right based upon their own merit to operate as a messenger of God. These people are not attitudinally self-righteous, self-seeking, stiff-necked, or hard of hearing. For the most part, they honestly just want to serve God and his people minus the politicking and self-posturing. Although this may be the case, even some of the best of us are tricked by the adversary's temptation to be reckless in our hearts and, subsequently, with our mouths. And it is at those moments wherein the Holy Spirit does what he does best, that is, convicts us of sin and leads us into the truth.

CHAPTER 4

WORDS OF RETALIATION

> "Not rendering evil for evil, or railing for railing, but contrariwise blessing, knowing that ye are thereunto called that ye should inherit a blessing."
> -1 Peter 3:9

I have spoken generally about our tendency to get back at people who have offended us, but now, perhaps, I will go into more detail about retaliation with another biblical illustration. In Genesis, we hear that Cain became jealous of his brother Abel and killed him because God received Abel's offering and not his. Cain acted out his frustration with God by killing someone who was born for his adversity (Proverbs 17:17).

That is just like the devil; he will cause some of us to demonize those who have our best interests in mind just because it seems like God favors them more than He does us. This is a core issue with many ministers that compels them to piss in God's sanctuary. They feel the need to denigrate or to disregard other believers or ministers to make them feel like decent servants of the Lord.

I have heard of ministers who were supposed to offer remarks about the preached Word for the evening say things like, "I pray that God gives me a portion of what you have." "I could not have touched that sermon with a ten-foot pole." "Don't do too much." "You'll never get on my level. The only way you will get on my level is that I die and you surpass me." People cannot celebrate what they are intimidated by or do not understand, and so they personalize the ministries of others. When offended ministers sense that they cannot walk in someone else's confirmed anointing, they dispel lies about a fellow minister to justify their heart of retaliation against God.

Being an offense to a fellow minister just for the simple reason of being all one can be in God is a dangerous situation. The offended minister may throw a brick at the unsuspecting minister over the pulpit. The offended minister may spread unfavorable lies amongst his circle of influence. Some ministers with senior authority may even try to keep other ministers in check by limiting their performances at such low levels of achievement—places where God has not intended for them to be. Abel suffered physically and died because of Cain's retaliation against God's decision to favor Abel's sacrifice and obedience, but many people today are not as lucky to die; they live in torment suffering emotionally and spiritually because of deathly jealousy amongst the brethren.

Certainly, God will not do us wrong, so if we ever find ourselves suffering injuries from fellow Christians, we should leave recompenses to God. The pulpit is not the place for us to defend ourselves. God said in His word, "'Vengeance is mine,' saith the Lord. 'I will repay'" (Romans 12:19b). God is a good record-keeper and he will make right every wrong. He will straighten the crooked places. Do not worry about being wronged. Instead of wasting time devising retaliatory plans against those who attacked us, we should use our time to work on ourselves and prepare for the future. God has our situations covered.

God's Word states, "Be not deceived. God is not mocked for whatsoever you sew that shall you also reap" (Galatians 6:7). We should make sure that through the process of change we are sewing the right seeds. We should make sure that our thoughts are pure towards God and his people. He said that suicide is to be preferred than to mess over the "least of these" (Matthew 18:6). It becomes fairly obvious in our congregations who the "least of these are." They are the poor, oppressed, uneducated, immature in faith and experience, etc. The urge to get back at people is compulsive and hinges on the premises that something is owed to the individual. Such is not the case. We have a right to be obedient to the will of the Father and receive blessings because of our obedience.

Possible Recourses to Retaliation

    1. *Make your election sure.*

Make sure that you are saved. Be very sure that you have confessed with your mouth, "Jesus is Lord," believed in your heart that He died on the cross for your sins, rose from the dead, and shall return someday soon with your reward in His hands. Receive the baptism of the Holy Spirit, He who is the down payment for your salvation. Knowledge of and belief in your salvation will ever keep you in the right frame of mind: humility.

2. *Make full proof of your ministry.*

Make sure that you have been called to do what you are doing and that you are not doing it because 1) It is cool. 2) Everyone in the family is doing it. 3) It promises prestige, power, and money. Do well and wait for God to silence your critics. The signs and the wonders will follow those who believe and have been called to do a specific work. No amount of gossip or sabotage can devastate a true word from God. It may be a hard fight, but the Word of the Lord will prevail in your life.

3. *Focus on your own ministry and personal development.*

Stop comparing yourself to other people. Be all God has called and anointed you to be. *The gifts and anointing God has bestowed upon the body of Christ were not meant to facilitate competition but cooperation.* Develop your gift through practice. Increase your anointing through inner submission. People who are jealous of you will project their disease on you in order to prevent the light of God from exposing the intents of their hearts, but do not believe them. Mind what God has given you and seek experts as well as resources that can make you be a better you for Christ's sake. Do not become weary and start pissing in God's sanctuary when certain people refuse to help you in your assignment. Sometimes you will just be a conflict of interest. Get over it and move on.

4. *Give God what He wants.*

Get in the lane God placed you and stay there until you receive further instructions. Unmercifully execute His will. Do not concern yourself with the opinions of others. You are to respect authority and those who have walked before you, but you have your own path to take. Never downplay what God has given you in order to pacify the fragile egos of those who should be mature and accomplished enough to embrace the ministry of another. God wants different things out of each of us, and we will move him to anger trying to replicate the ministry of another. Represent well the mold out of which God fashioned your spirit and soul.

The dream that I shared in the introduction of this book showed that a fire ensued after I pissed in the sanctuary. Certainly, words of retaliation elicit the fleshly desire to fight, but quarreling should not be found amongst the people of God. Jesus taught us that the love we share for one another proves that we are children of God (John 13:35). With the fruit of love comes the ability to just let some offenses be.

CHAPTER 5

SYMPATHY- SEEKING WORDS OF BITTERNESS

> "Looking diligent lest any man fail of the grace of God ; lest any root of bitterness springing up , causing trouble and by it, defiling many."
>
> -Hebrews 12:15

A lot of times we think that people have taken things away from us, but in actuality, they have not. The Scripture teaches, "the blessings of the Lord makes rich and adds no sorrow" (Proverbs 10:22). In other words, when we wait for God to gift us, we will not be sorry for having what we have. We may get attacked for possessing His power and material, but we will fully and inwardly appreciate his gifting, recognizing it as a source of our well-being and identity. It will make up for any slack we have in our lives and give us the power to live. When I think of bitterness and sympathy, I think of Esau, who for one morsel of meat sold his birthright to his brother (Hebrews 12:16). He did not value what his father had given him. Oftentimes, we disregard what God has given us and let it go, but when someone else picks up the opportunity or anointing, we become jealous. We get jealous because we see the manifested power and glory in the lives of others who pick up what we have willfully placed down out of laziness or rebellion.

The Letter to the Hebrews tells us that Esau sought a place for repentance, but he could not find one. Give thanks to God, because we can repent today. Give thanks to God, because our past failures do not have the power to devastate God's will to prosper our lives. If you laid down and treated disrespectfully what God has bestowed upon you, repent now. Receive the forgiveness of God and pick up where you have left off. Do not sit at a place of bitterness thinking that your colaborers have stolen your shine. No—they have worked with what you cast away as a trifle. Instead of using your mouth to downplay what God is doing through them, learn how to rightly handle your anointing and God-given opportunities.

The next time the enemy tempts you to become bitter and sympathy-seeking in the face of a brother's success or elevation, ask yourself the following questions: 1) Who gave me my anointing? 2) Who gave the influence I have in the lives of others? 3) Who gave me this opportunity? Upon asking these questions, you will acknowledge the centrality of Christ in your life and you can declare like the saints of old, "This that I have the world didn't give and the world can't take away." Any anointing or opportunity that God has graced you with, you can pick it up and operate in it when you have a mind to be obedient, for gifts are truly bestowed without repentance (Romans 11:29). We are not living in a dispensation in which we can cry for an opportunity for repentance and not find it. People who think the opposite are the ones who use their mouths to tear down a fellow brother. Wrongly perceiving that they have no hope, they become bitter and seek sympathy from others by dispelling exactly what they think of another for having allegedly robbed them.

Possible Recourses to Sympathy-Seeking Words of Bitterness

1. *Honor the gifts and opportunities God has given you.*

Fight to keep what God has given you. A life of integrity and hard work is the safeguard that is necessary to preserve the holiness of what God has entrusted into your care. No man, woman, habit, or addiction should compromise what God has placed in your hands. At the end of the day, the ruling question that you should ponder in your heart concerning your ministry is: What really matters? Make decisions based upon what matters the most in your life.

2. *Repent and receive God's forgiveness for treating lightly what God has graced you with.*

A lot of people want to skip the process of repentance. It is a big thing that can be accomplished within seconds. Some procrastinate in repenting, because sometimes it is painful and embarrassing to do so. However, emotional pain is a part of the suffering for our disobedience; repentance is the only authentic, immediate response to disobedience. It may be embarrassing, but Jesus is not embarrassed. He takes pleasure in feeling his children turn from their wicked ways. Our humility before His presence shows that we respect His fathering and recognize that we live by His grace and not by the law.

3. *Observe someone who respects and takes seriously what God has placed in his hands.*

The Bible teaches us to "mark that perfect man and behold the upright: for the end of that man is peace" (Psalm 34:37). We ought to have peace in doing what God has anointed us to do. If you recognize that there is scandal concerning that area God has gifted and anointed you, recognize that you are under satanic attack. Be free in who you are in God. If that means you have to observe others, do so to get that extra boost of confidence. Upon looking at their lives, you will hear in your spirit the idea, "If they can do all of this through My power, what more can you do if you will just trust and obey Me?" Know that the Holy Spirit is communicating this idea. You have what it takes to do what God is leading you to do.

Do not forget the scriptural witness concerning this very thing. Remember that the angel of the Lord directed

Mary to consider her cousin Elizabeth who had conceived a child in her old age and after she had been barren for years. The angel directed her to that witness to increase her own confidence in the sure word of the Lord for her life—that she could give birth to the Son of God through the power of the Holy Spirit without the aid of a man (Luke 1:36). That is one of our problems. We mistakenly think that we cannot do what God has anointed us to do without man's help. We should not put our trust in people. We need God, and God will touch the hearts of men to help us get the job done.

4. *Use your opportunities to grow and not complain.*

All is not lost. Trust and believe that God is not through using you yet. Your purpose and influence will not run out as long as you shall live. No matter who you are or what you have done, God still wants to use you to show someone the way. He still wants to use you to glorify His holy name. Why hold something against yourself when

God has clearly forgiven you and released his power in your life? Get up and keep it moving.

Think back again to the dream that I shared in the introduction of this book. Despite all that I had gone through, God was still moving in my ministry. The people who were connected to me were flowing in the Spirit of God and receiving the benefits of knowing Him. All was going well until I pissed in the sanctuary. Learn from this dream. Despite the failures and difficulties of your life, God is still moving in your life. He is moving when it looks like He is doing nothing. Do not mess up this next move of God in your life. Just trust Him and focus on the assignment at hand.

CHAPTER 6

WORDS OF MIND CONTROL

"...Let every man be fully persuaded in his own mind."
-Romans 14:5

Pissing in God's sanctuary with the intent of controlling other people's thoughts and emotions is a detrimentally deliberate act that is sheer rebellion to the Spirit of God. Just because you have an issue with someone that does not give you the right to use your authority in the lives of others to make your issues with another the issues of your audience members. Do not get me wrong; if you know something about someone that can potentially damage the reputation or safety of someone who is accountable to you, it is within your right to safeguard his anointing and life by sharing with him pertinent information about another. However, simple, personal offenses should not be shared so as to affect the mind and mood of your subordinate against your offender.

How often does this happen in the body of Christ! Ministers know that those who support them quite naturally possess a Petrine spirit. Their supporters are willing to cut off the ear of anyone who opposes them, and ministers use this knowledge to piss on them about what others have done to them so as to blacklist the offender. This is not the Spirit of Christ! The Bible teaches us that at the end of the day, everyone should have the liberty to think for himself. Let the truth prevail without a personal skewing of it. The truth of the matter is that when offenses are recounted one by one, he will not fully disclose his full involvement in the issue. It is wise for one not to let someone else's issues become his. We should strive to maintain the bond of peace, speak the same thing, and glorify Christ.

Possible Recourses to Words of Mind Control

1. *Examine yourself.*

Make sure that the spirit that motivates your speech is the Spirit of Christ and not the spirit of man or the adversary. Christ is a compassionate, loving, and forgiving God. At times we are the complete opposite, but recognition of this fact is good material to begin a prayer of repentance.

2. *Let love be your guide.*

Think not only about your best interests, but also, think about the interests of those who have offended you. They still have to live and do a work for God. Sometimes it is not about being right but more so about being effective. We are all servants of the Lord who want to be used by God. Think gently about one another, for Jesus Himself said that it was by the love we have for one another that unbelievers can receive our Christ narrative (John 13:35).

3. *Let people think for themselves.*

As ministers of the gospel, our job is to preach Christ lived, died, rose, and is coming again. Also, we have the task of expounding upon the whole counsel of God in light of the gospel. In doing so, we ought to model for people how to think reasonably based upon facts. We ought to model for them how to "hear the conclusion of the whole matter" (Ecclesiastes 12:13). If you are not willing to divest yourself of God's anointing and opportunities because of your involvement in the offense, do not use God's platform to present a skewed account that seeks to do the same to someone else. Heaven is listening. Your words will either justify or condemn you (Matthew 12:37).

Think again back to the dream that I shared with you in the introduction. When I entered the sanctuary, I did not say a word, but my actions had great ramifications. My gesture had the efficacy to derail an authentic move of God. When you consider your words, remember that actions speak louder than they do. What you do not say may have greater effect than what you do say; therefore, rule your body well. Make it obey the gospel of Jesus Christ lest you influence people to think and behave in ungodly ways in response to your mind controlling agenda.

FINAL WORDS

I exhort you to preach the word in season and out of season! Speak what Christ tells you to speak whether people like it or not. Yield your body to the full service of the One who called you to be His witnesses to the uttermost parts of the world. Just be very sure your words are spirit and life. Be very sure you are not making light of this holy opportunity to speak on God's behalf by trying to assassinate people's character or weaken their witness in the world. Be sure your words restore the ones who fall from grace.

When I was a little boy, the Spirit of God spoke to my father in a vision. The Spirit said, "I will not have my children to eat from a broken plate." Ministers are as saucers from which God's precious lambs eat life-giving sustenance. Before ministers can bring about life for others, they must first receive it for themselves. If we will not yield to the Holy Spirit and allow him to mend our brokenness, we will inadvertently or even purposely spill glass into the Word of God, making it of no effect. Glass was not meant to be eaten. The broken pieces of our lives were not meant to be our nourishment. They were meant to be a platform to proclaim life. Don't mess up this holy opportunity!

God has favored you and entrusted you with his holy work of engrafting souls in the Kingdom. Put your best foot forward. Remain positive. Do not be sidetracked by the many offenses that shall come your way. Pray for those you seek to serve so your heart can be pure before them, for people feel you before they hear you. Recognize the sanctity of every moment you wake up and serve as a representative of Christ.

Take off your carnality; do not piss in God's sanctuary. This is holy ground. Everywhere you are is holy ground—a sacred place permeated with the Spirit of God. It is God's will to use your body as a living sacrifice that demonstrates the power of God unto salvation, the reconciliatory gospel of Jesus Christ. When you are affronted for the name of Christ, hide beneath His wings. He is coming to judge the wicked and receive the righteous unto Himself. In His hand shall be your reward. Be strong and finish well what Jesus has started. May the zeal of the Holy Ghost burn in your soul and the wisdom of Christ guide your steps! Fresh wind! Fresh fire!

CONCLUDING PRAYER

Let's conclude this reading by reciting Psalm 26 together in prayer.

Dear Heavenly Father,

[1](*A PSALM* of David.) Judge me, O LORD; for I have walked in mine integrity: I have trusted also in the LORD; *THEREFORE* I shall not slide.[2] Examine me, O LORD, and prove me; try my reins and my heart. [3] For thy lovingkindness *IS* before mine eyes: and I have walked in thy truth.[4] I have not sat with vain persons, neither will I go in with dissemblers. [5] I have hated the congregation of evil doers; and will not sit with the wicked. [6] I will wash mine hands in innocency: so will I compass thine altar, O LORD:[7] That I may publish with the voice of thanksgiving, and tell of all thy wondrous works. [8] LORD, I have loved the habitation of thy house, and the place where thine honour dwelleth. [9] Gather not my soul with sinners, nor my life with bloody men:[10] In whose hands *IS* mischief, and their right hand is full of bribes.[11] But as for me, I will walk in mine integrity: redeem me, and be merciful unto me.[12] My foot standeth in an even place: in the congregations will I bless the LORD.

In Jesus' Name,

Amen

ABOUT THE AUTHOR

Pastor Cederick L. Moore is the founder and senior pastor of *Spirit & Truth Cathedral of Fire*, an independent, fledgling congregation in Washington, NC. A native of Chocowinity, North Carolina, Moore has lived a fairly secluded life in the rural parts of Beaufort County. At a young age, Moore learned to distinguish the voice of God, examine the Word, and serve God in His sanctuary. He is a servant of the Lord who cares about the quality of life and spiritual well-being of all people. He makes deliberate efforts to touch the world with the unadulterated gospel of the Lord Jesus Christ and challenges believers to grow up in Christ in all things. By the grace of God and tutelage of the Holy Spirit, Moore delivers seasoned words that speak to the issues of the heart. It is his life ambition to preach the gospel with boldness, clarity, and power to the ends of the world with the expectation of preparing the hearts of thousands to ten thousands for the Second Coming of the Lord Jesus Christ.

Pastor Moore understands and appreciates the role that education plays in the social, psychological, and spiritual development of people. He attended the Beaufort County Schools and graduated from Southside High School in June 2006 with honors. After high school, he attended the University of North Carolina at Chapel Hill and majored in English and minored in Christianity and Culture. After his undergraduate career, he enrolled in and completed the Master Teacher Fellows Program at Wake

Forest University. When he is not ministering or studying, he teaches English at a local high school. Moore is a finisher and he seeks to obtain knowledge and skills necessary to enhance the quality of life and spiritual well-being for him and those entrusted to his care.

It does not yet appear to the world what he shall be in the Kingdom of God, but Moore knows who he is in God and where it is He is taking him. He is a man of eternal vision, faith, hope, love, holiness, order, and excellence. He believes that changed lives prove effective ministry and consistency produces results. Pray for him as he goes forth in the strength of the Lord—pray that he continues to grow and produce fruit to the glory of the Father.

Write to Pastor Cederick L. Moore at:

P.O. Box 636
Chocowinity, NC 27817

Is there a book inside of you? Ever wanted to self publish but didn't know how? Concerned about the financial part of self publishing? Relax. Take a deep breath. We can help!

Finally! An affordable Self Publishing company for all of your Self Publishing needs. We have the right services, with the right prices with the right quality. So, what are you waiting for?

Unpack those dreams, break out that pen, your dreams of getting published may not be so far off after all!

Jasher Press & Co. is here to provide you with Consulting, Book Formatting, Cover Designs, editing services but most importantly inspiration to bring your dreams to past.

And this whole process can be done in less than 90 days! You thought about it, you talked about it but now is the time!

WWW.JASHERPRESS.COM
1-888-220-2068
CUSTOMERSERVICE@JASHERPRESS.COM

www.ingramcontent.com/pod-product-compliance
Lightning Source LLC
LaVergne TN
LVHW020938090426
835512LV00020B/3413